Samson's Titanic Journey belongs to:

Campbell Adamson.

Christmas 2019 from
auntie Elaine +
Uncle Willie xxx.

For Taryn and Rowan with love
- Lauren

For Mum and Dad
- Roisin

For Roslyn, Ben, Rachael and Snuffles
- Bernard

Text copyright © 2004 Lauren Graham
Illustrations copyright © 2004 Roisin Mathews

Published in Ireland by O'Donnell Press,
12 Coolemoyne Park, Jordanstown, Co. Antrim BT37 0RP
Telephone: 028 9096 6493
Email address: b.odonnell93@ntlworld.com

First published by O'Donnell Press, 2004
This edition, June 2018

A CIP catalogue record of this book is available from the British Library.

Printed in Ireland by GPS Colour Graphics Ltd.
Repro Scanning by iris colour.

ISBN 0-9546163-5-9

8 9 10

Samson's Titanic Journey

By Lauren Graham
Illustrated by Roisin Mathews

O'DONNELL PRESS

Samson was so excited. He had lived in the shipyard in Belfast since he was a baby mouse but never before had as much fuss been made about a ship. The beautiful new luxury liner called Titanic was about to be launched. The shipyard workers had been building it for months and now the day had arrived when it would finally set sail for Southampton.

Samson was going too. He had decided to leave his hometown in search of a better life in America and couldn't think of a more spectacular way to get there than by travelling on board the Titanic.

As the final preparations for the launch were put in place, Samson slipped stealthily aboard. He watched the excited spectators waving madly from the docks as Titanic sailed splendidly down Belfast Lough.

Once Titanic had travelled
out to sea, Samson found a cosy
little corner close to one of the
huge ship's boilers, unpacked his
belongings and unrolled his pretty
patchwork blanket. Snuggled
securely in his new bed, he fell
fast asleep.

It didn't seem long before they
reached Southampton. Again there
was a huge buzz of excitement as
many passengers began to board
Titanic. Samson was no longer alone
in the boiler room. Other rats and
mice had arrived on board and
began to settle down for the long
journey to America. There was
lots of noise and fuss so Samson
decided to go out on deck to get
some fresh air.

Titanic was just about to set sail on her maiden voyage to America. Hundreds of people had gathered to watch and wave. Fancy cars were being lifted on board and ladies in beautiful bouncy bonnets were promenading along the decks. Samson ran as fast as he could to the top of the ship and hid behind the fourth funnel in an effort to get the best view.

The ship's horn sounded and Titanic was on her way.
She glided effortlessly through the glistening waves and
after two brief stops to pick up more passengers in France
and Ireland, she journeyed across the Atlantic Ocean,
on her way to America.

Now there was nothing more for Samson to do but discover Titanic herself. He decided to start his exploration at the top of the ship. This was where the first class cabins could be found. As he was scampering around, he became aware of a delicious smell wafting through the air. Samson's tummy began to rumble. In all the excitement, he had missed lunch. Samson followed the aroma and it led him to the dining room. He had never before seen such grandeur. Crystal chandeliers shone brightly on the dark, rich wooden panelling. Tall gentlemen in top hats led elegant ladies in long, swirling skirts as they swished down the magnificent staircase into the grand dining room.

Crisp linen tablecloths were set
with silver cutlery and sumptuous
food. Samson's mouth began to
water. He slipped, unseen under the
tables and nibbled leftovers and
crumbs until his tummy ached.
Then he climbed to the top of the
staircase, hid inside the majestic
clock and drifted to sleep listening
to the sounds of the string quartet.

A few days later, as Samson was relaxing in his bed in the boiler room, he heard some of the other rats and mice talking excitedly. They were planning to attend a party in the third class section of the ship. Samson decided that he would join them.

When he arrived, the party was in full swing. The deck was crowded. Cheerful chattering and laughter could be heard above the lively fiddle music. Passengers were dancing to the sounds of reels and jigs while others relaxed with a drink, happily watching the performances. Samson soon found the other mice gathered together in a corner and he too joined in the fun.

It was very late when he returned to
his bed in the boiler room. He hadn't
been sleeping for long when he was
woken by a loud crash and the ship
creaked to a sudden halt. Samson was
scared. He knew that something was
wrong. He scampered outside to find
out what was happening. Shattered
ice slipped and slid across the deck.
Titanic had hit an iceberg.

When he returned to the boiler
room, Samson discovered to his
dismay that it had already begun to
fill with water. Titanic was sinking.
Rats and mice were running to higher
ground in an effort to escape. Samson
followed them.

Lots of panicking passengers had now arrived on deck. Everyone wanted to board the lifeboats but it was clear that there was not enough room for them all. Women and children clambered on board and one by one the lifeboats were lowered into the sea. As he watched the last lifeboat disappear, Samson knew that he was in trouble. He had no way of escape. Titanic was plunging head first into the Atlantic Ocean.

Samson was so frightened. He didn't want to end up like a drowned rat. He wrapped his tail tightly round the ship's railings and held on for all he was worth. Suddenly there was an earth shattering sound as Titanic split in two. Samson felt as if his heart was in his mouth when the rear of the ship plummeted into the sea. For a moment, the force of the impact dragged Samson underwater. His little legs paddled fiercely and with immense effort he reached the ocean's surface. Gasping for breath, he swam through the icy waters towards a piece of driftwood. He lay on top, shivering with fear and cold and listening to the screams and whistles of Titanic's passengers as they pleaded for help. No one came and it wasn't long before the panic was replaced by an eerie silence.

It was two hours before another ship called the Carpathia appeared. By that time, it was too late for many of the passengers. Samson was one of the lucky ones. He used all his energy to climb off the driftwood and onto the Carpathia. Confused and frightened, he hid between some old rope in a corner of the deck and stayed there for several days until the ship docked in New York. Unlike lots of others, he had been rescued and lived to tell his tale.

He could now begin his new life in America. But Samson knew that however exciting his future would be, he would never forget his Titanic journey.